SPECTRUM READERS

UNUSUAL!
Ocean Life

By Teresa Domnauer

Carson-Dellosa
Publishing

An imprint of Carson-Dellosa Publishing, LLC
P.O. Box 35665
Greensboro, NC 27425-5665

carsondellosa.com

Printed in the USA. All rights reserved.
ISBN 978-1-4838-0133-9

01-002141120

Earth's oceans are full of weird and
wonderful animals.
Some have hard shells, and others have
spiky coverings.
Some are well hidden, and others have
bold colors or stripes.
Marine animals move around, feed, and
interact in fascinating ways.
Keep reading to learn about these
unusual creatures of the deep.

Jellyfish

Graceful jellyfish drift along ocean currents and waves.

They propel themselves by spitting water.

A jellyfish is an *invertebrate*, or an animal without a backbone.

A jellyfish's soft, bell-shaped body can be colorful or clear and is filled with jelly.

Jellyfish catch small sea animals with their stinging tentacles.

Fun Facts

- Ninety-five percent of all animals are invertebrates.
- Jellyfish were around before the dinosaurs, millions of years ago.

Sea Anemone

Sea anemones look like flowers, but they are actually animals.

These colorful creatures are relatives of jellyfish and coral.

Sea anemones rarely move.

They attach to rocks or coral reefs.

Tentacles around an anemone's mouth are filled with poison.

These tentacles help the animal catch fish and other prey.

Fun Facts

- There are about 1,000 kinds of anemones.

- Clownfish (like the one shown) have a special outer layer that protects them from anemone stings.

Sea Urchin

Sea urchins are invertebrates that have a spiny covering.
They come in many shapes and colors and are relatives of starfish.
There are nearly 1,000 kinds of sea urchins found all over the world.
Sea urchins live on rocks and hard surfaces of the ocean floor.
Tiny ocean plants called *algae* are a favorite food for urchins.

Fun Facts

- Some sea urchins lay several million eggs at a time!
- Urchins "see" by detecting light with their spines.

Soft Coral

Coral look like pretty plants.
But, they are invertebrates related to
anemones and jellyfish.
There are two kinds of coral: soft coral
and stony coral.
Soft coral have skeletons on the inside of
their bodies.
Stony coral have skeletons on the outside.
Coral attach to hard surfaces like rocks or
sunken ships.

Fun Facts

- Over 200 kinds of coral make up the Great Barrier Reef in Australia.
- Coral get their bright colors from the different kinds of algae that they eat.

Coral Reef

Coral reefs form habitats for thousands of ocean species.
Reefs are found close to the surface in warm tropical waters.
They are built from layers of stony coral skeletons over thousands of years.
Pollution and climate change threaten these fragile habitats.
When sea temperatures get too warm, coral can become sick and die.

Fun Facts

- Coral reefs cover a small part of the ocean floor, but they are home to one-quarter of all ocean creatures!
- Some coral reefs began growing millions of years ago.

13

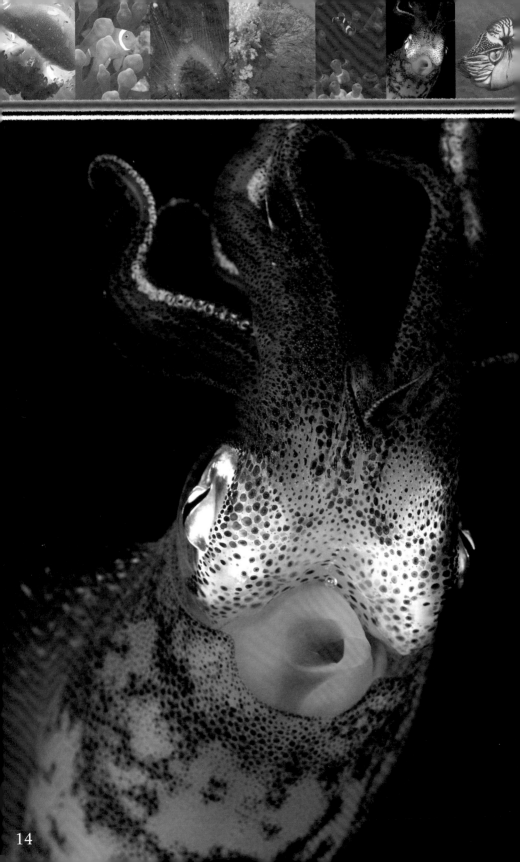

Squid

Squid are part of the mollusk family. Most mollusks, like snails and clams, have shells that cover their soft bodies. Squid have shells, too, but they are inside of their bodies! A squid has a total of ten arms. Two arms are long tentacles with suckers. When in danger, squid squirt dark ink to confuse enemies.

Fun Facts

- The giant squid is the largest invertebrate on the planet.
- A squid's eye is very similar to a human eye.

Chambered Nautilus

This sea creature is a chambered nautilus. Like the squid, it is also a mollusk. The chambered nautilus gets its name from the small sections, or chambers, inside it.

As it grows, more chambers get added to its coiled shell.

The nautilus has over 90 tentacles around its mouth that it uses to catch prey.

Fun Facts

- The chambered nautilus has been around for 200 million years.
- These mollusks eject water to propel themselves backward.

Mantis Shrimp

Shrimp are part of the crustacean family. Crustaceans are animals that have skeletons on the outside of their bodies, jointed legs, and antennae. A shrimp sheds its skeleton as it grows. A new skeleton grows in its place. Shrimp are able to swim backward. The mantis shrimp has very strong claws for catching prey.

Fun Facts

- The mantis shrimp can grow to 12 inches long—that's as long as your ruler.

- The mantis shrimp has 16 cones in each eye, allowing it to see many more colors than humans do.

Spiny Lobster

The lobster is another member of the crustacean family.

Lobsters are found all over the world.

They crawl along the ocean floor.

Lobsters have five pairs of legs and large claws called *pincers*.

Most are nocturnal, which means they are active at night.

They dine on fish, mollusks, and seaweed.

Fun Facts

- The largest lobster ever caught weighed 44 pounds and was over three feet long. It may have been 100 years old!

- Spiny lobsters do not have large claws like other lobsters.

Lionfish

The striped lionfish is a popular fish for home aquariums.
In the ocean, its stripes help it blend in with its coral reef habitat.
The bold red and white stripes warn predators to stay away.
Lionfish have up to 18 feathery fins. They use their fins to "herd" schools of fish into small spaces so they can be caught more easily.

Fun Facts

- A lionfish's fins produce venom.
- Lionfish have also been called *dragon fish*, *scorpion fish*, and *turkey fish*!

Parrot Fish

Brightly colored parrot fish also live among coral reefs.

Parrot fish have "beaks" which they use to scrape algae and soft coral from reefs. Special teeth in their throats help parrot fish grind their food.

Parrot fish can grow to 45 pounds—that's the size of a first-grader!

Fun Facts

- Parrot fish have a wide variety of colors and patterns.

- Eighty kinds of parrot fish are found in tropical waters around the world.

Grouper

The massive grouper is a member of the bass fish family.

It has a large mouth and a heavy body, growing up to 500 pounds.

That's about the weight of a motorcycle!

Green and brown in color, grouper live in warm seas and prefer to stay hidden.

They are valued in many places as food.

Fun Facts

- A grouper can change its colors and patterns for camouflage.
- The smallest grouper is the coney. It is reddish gray with blue spots.

Stingray

Stingrays are relatives of sharks.
Unlike sharks, stingrays are inactive most
of the time.
They hide on the sandy ocean floor.
Stingrays have flattened bodies with eyes
on the tops of their heads.
Their nostrils, mouths, and gills are
underneath.
Stingrays swim gracefully by rippling
their wing-like sides.

Fun Facts

- Stingrays have venomous spines, but they are used only for protection.

- Sensors around a stingray's mouth help it find prey such as worms and mollusks.

Humpback Whale

There are two kinds of whales: toothed whales and baleen whales.
The humpback whale is a baleen whale. Baleen whales do not have teeth.
Instead, they have a special filter called a *baleen* inside their mouths.
The baleen catches tiny sea creatures such as krill and plankton.
These massive sea mammals can weigh 40 tons—that's as much as 40 cars!

Fun Facts

- Humpback whales leap out of the water, then splash down with a powerful slap. This is called *breaching*.

- Humpback whales are known for the song-like sounds they make.

UNUSUAL! Ocean Life Comprehension Questions

1. How do you think the parrot fish got its name?

2. What do a lionfish's stripes tell other fish?

3. What do sea urchins like to eat?

4. How do sea anemones catch their prey?

5. Name three sea creatures that are invertebrates.

6. What is a baleen? What is it used for?

7. How many arms does a squid have?

8. Name two types of coral.

9. What threatens coral reefs?

10. Describe the body of a stingray.

11. What does *nocturnal* mean?

12. How does a nautilus catch prey?

13. Name two mollusks.

14. How many legs does a lobster have?